The Open University

Education:
a second-level
course

BLOCK 3 TEACHING AND LEARNING

UNIT 2

TEACHING

Prepared for the Course Team by Peter Woods

EXPLORING EDUCATIONAL *ISSUES*

ACKNOWLEDGEMENTS

Grateful acknowledgement is made to the following sources for permission to reproduce material in this unit.

Text

DES (1982) *The New Teacher in School*, © Crown Copyright. Reproduced with the permission of the Controller of Her Majesty's Stationery Office; Broadhead, P. (1987) 'A blueprint for the good teacher? The HMI/DES model of good primary practice', *British Journal of Educational Studies*, **35**(1), February 1987, Basil Blackwell Ltd; Mac an Ghaill, M. (1992) 'Teachers' work: curriculum restructuring, culture, power and comprehensive schooling', *British Journal of Sociology of Education*, **13**(2), pp. 177–99, Carfax Publishing Company.

Cartoons

page 8: Cartoon by Bill Stott, *Education*, 19 October 1984, p. 315, Pitman Publishing, reproduced by kind permission of Bill Stott; *page 10 (top)*: Cartoon by Roy Mitchell, *Education*, 7 June 1985, p. 512, Pitman Publishing, reproduced by kind permission of Roy Mitchell; *page 10 (bottom)*: Cartoon by Roy Mitchell, *Education*, 4 July 1986, p. 9, Pitman Publishing, reproduced by kind permission of Roy Mitchell; *page 15*: Cartoon by Bill Stott, *Education*, 10 October 1980, p. 355, Pitman Publishing, reproduced by kind permission of Bill Stott; *page 17*: David McKee; *page 36*: Allan Gardham.

The Open University, Walton Hall, Milton Keynes MK7 6AA

First published 1995

Edited, designed and typeset by The Open University

Printed in the United Kingdom by Page Bros (Norwich) Ltd

ISBN 0 7492 4588 3

This unit forms part of an Open University course. The complete list of blocks is printed at the end of each unit. If you have not enrolled on the course and would like to buy this or other Open University material, please write to Open University Educational Enterprises Ltd, 12 Cofferidge Close, Stony Stratford MK11 1BY, United Kingdom. If you wish to enquire about enrolling as an Open University student please write to The Admissions Office, The Open University, PO Box 48, Walton Hall, Milton Keynes MK7 6AB, United Kingdom.

1.1

CONTENTS

HOW TO STUDY THIS UNIT

The aims of the unit are to consider the nature of teaching and to look at two main approaches to examining it. These are: (a) what I term an 'official' view, seen in reports from the Department of Education and Science (DES)[1], Her Majesty's Inspectorate (HMI) and the Office for Standards in Education (OFSTED); and (b) sociological approaches concerned with the study of social factors influencing teacher activity.

There is a vast literature on teaching, especially 'effective teaching', which I have made no attempt to review. Rather, I have selected from some of the more prominent studies of the day, across the range indicated. You will be able to compare and contrast these different approaches, to study each in some depth, and also to evaluate them in terms of their thoroughness, appropriateness and research methodology.

The current educational issue here is the 'quality of teaching', which has received increasing political attention in recent years – hence the succession of reports discussed in Section 2. This unit, however, is not just about 'good teaching' or 'effective teaching', though there will be quite a lot of mentions of these, since identifying the conditions for good or effective teaching was the aim of many of the studies. 'Good teaching' and 'bad teaching', whatever these may be, have to be seen within the full context of what teachers do. You have to have some understanding of why teachers act as they do before any realistic prescriptions can be made about what they should do. It is this broad understanding that this unit seeks to provide.

By the time you have finished the unit you should be able to evaluate DES/HMI/OFSTED reports on teaching and to describe and assess critically some research studies on teachers' efficiency. You should understand the differences and similarities between official reports and social scientific research and you should have some knowledge of social factors that affect teachers' activities. You should also see the relevance of certain basic concepts, such as traditional and progressive teaching, teachers' values, commitment and strategies, school ethos and external constraints. Finally, you should be able to apply the knowledge and skills gained in the unit to current questions about teaching.

The activities within the text are an important part of your study of this unit. You should attempt each one as it occurs and before reading on.

---

[1]This has changed since, first to the Department for Education (DFE), and currently to the Department for Education and Employment (DFEE). Since the reports discussed in this unit were published by the DES, that title is retained here.

SET READING

The set readings for this unit are in:

WOODS, P. (ed.) *Contemporary Issues in Teaching and Learning* (Reader 2, Woods).

You will also be asked to refer to:

MACKINNON, D. and STATHAM, J. with HALES, M. (1995) *Education in the UK: facts and figures*, London, Hodder and Stoughton/The Open University (the Fact Book).

BROADCASTS AND CASSETTES

One television programme, *A School for Our Times?*, is associated specifically with this unit.

1 INTRODUCTION: ISSUES IN TEACHING

* There's too much letting children do what they like these days. Too much play and freedom and not enough instruction and discipline ...

Children are not made to learn things like they used to be. They leave school without knowing their tables or being able to spell or punctuate ...

Teachers have much better relationships with their pupils these days.

Teachers are born, not made.

Only ideas about teaching change. The practice remains the same.

Teaching is more of an art than a science.

The world is changing radically, and so is teaching.

There are limits to what an individual teacher can accomplish. For some, the mounting pressures have brought a great deal of stress.

Activity 1 (allow about 5 minutes) ————————————————

Study the above quotations, which are all comments on the current state of teaching. You might be able to add some of your own, or some you have heard from others, or read about. What are your own views about teachers and teaching today, compared, say, to when you were at school? Have things changed and, if so, in what respects? Have they been changes for the better or for the worse? To what do you attribute these changes, or lack of change if you feel there has been none?

What basic issues lie behind such views and statements?

1.1 There are a number of issues here. There is the question of what kind of teaching produces the most effective learning. Such a question is fraught with all manner of difficulty about definitions and criteria. How, for example, can you distinguish between different kinds of teaching? Over the past thirty years, much of the debate has characterized approaches in terms of a division between traditional and progressive teaching. This follows a general tendency to represent the considerable complexity involved in teaching under two broad, though not discrete, groups of educational discourse, variously characterized as child-centred versus teacher-centred, activity-oriented versus subject-matter oriented, democratic versus authoritarian, progressive versus traditional. You might relate the first two statements in the list above to forms of 'progressive' teaching and, indeed, there is a belief among some that this is responsible for lower standards (though this assumes there is agreement on what 'standards' are and how you can measure or assess them). Another difficulty is how to judge the effectiveness of different styles, assuming that you can identify them realistically.

1.2 From views of teaching seen in terms of broad groupings of behaviours and their products, some studies have turned to individual teachers and pupils, and the actual tasks upon which they are engaged. The focus here is on the pupil, as much as the teacher, and on the process (i.e. what actually occurs between teacher and pupil), rather than the product. Much is seen to depend on the quality of the tasks presented to pupils, judged by the extent to which these match the needs and abilities of pupils. This might be termed an 'opportunities to learn' model. A great deal of research has been done in this area, mainly by psychologists, notably on 'teaching styles', as in the work of Bennett (1976) and the ORACLE studies (for example, Galton, Simon and Croll, 1980); and on 'classroom tasks' by Bennett *et al.* (1984). These are important studies and undoubtedly contribute to a comprehensive understanding of teaching, though we do not have space in this unit to consider them. Rather, we concentrate on factors affecting teachers' ability to teach – what might be termed as an 'opportunities to *teach*' model. These derive partially from within the teacher, and partially from without. With regard to the former, since the teachers' action of the later 1980s and the reforms of the late 1980s and early 1990s, morale within the profession as a whole has been low. In Section 3 I shall consider questions of the individual teacher's values and commitment, and their implications for teaching.

1.3   With regard to factors deriving from outside the teacher, it is generally recognized that teaching and learning have to be seen within a social context. Classrooms and schools differ, as do subjects, and groups of children (depending on such things as age, sex, numbers, neighbourhood). There are differences, too, among local education authorities on policy and on the provision of resources. Teachers may be subject to parental pressure (e.g. being strongly for or against a particular reform); and teachers have to operate within the general provisions, policies and principles put out by the government of the day. These, then, are all constraints on a teacher's activity. They exert pressure to operate in certain directions and against others, and must be taken into account for a full appreciation of the possibilities of what teachers might accomplish (see Section 4 for this). I shall begin, however, with a consideration of what might be termed the 'official' view of good teaching. A series of publications in the 1980s from the DES had a lot to say about how teaching should be done. The same principles have re-appeared in more recent publications (OFSTED, 1992; 1994). I shall examine the assumptions behind these prescriptions.

1.4   By the end of the unit, if not exactly in a position to provide definitive answers to the questions raised (the area of study is not one that lends itself readily to such solutions), we should, nevertheless, have clarified the questions and evaluated some contrasting approaches to tackling them.

Activity 2   (allow about 5 minutes) ————————————————
You must have some ideas of your own as to what makes a 'good' teacher. Jot down the criteria that, from your experience, seem to you to be important (think of knowledge, teaching skills, relationships, classroom management, etc.). Do you know any teacher who consistently combines all the elements you have listed?

————————————————————————————————————

1.5 How difficult did you find Activity 2? I actually found it very difficult, for a number of reasons. One was that, having listed several attributes (knowledge of subject matter, ability to explain, good motivation of pupils and so on), I was not sure that in putting them all together I had a 'good teacher' or a 'Frankenstein's monster' of one. This may be due in part to another concern and that is the difficulty of definition. What do we mean, for example, by 'ability to explain'? Is it innate or learned? Is it applied and, if so, is it applied equally among all children? Who judges the adequacy of the explanation and by what criteria? Are the explanations well-founded? In what kind of school is the teacher working (there are several key aspects to that), in what kind of society, at what point in history … and so on. Each quality seems to beg a whole new range of questions.

1.6 The inadequacy of some commonsense definitions might be further illustrated by some examples of reputedly 'good' teaching that I have come across at various times, some of which are clearly nothing of the sort.

- A teacher who likes, at his 'best', to put on a 'performance' in his lessons. This was personally satisfying for him, but left his pupils unmoved.
- Some pupils once thought a teacher 'very good', because, it materialized, he was so incomprehensible they thought him on a higher plane of knowledge than ordinary mortals.
- Some teachers have been considered 'good' because they keep order amongst their pupils, regardless of the methods they use, or what they actually teach.

1.7 Some have based their judgement on particular aspects of teaching, while leaving other important aspects out of account. These might include those who claim 'relationships' are all important and who assume that 'outcomes' will then follow. On the other hand, Roehler and Duffy (1986) begin an article with the sentence: 'It is intuitively sensible that the most effective teachers are those who are good at explaining curricular content.' As mentioned above, there are problems with such a statement. Again there are those who claim that teaching is primarily an art that defies analysis, which would perhaps account for all the above difficulties. Those who argue that 'teachers are born not made' would presumably subscribe to such a view, putting their success down to an indefinable charisma. Hartley (1985, p. 113), for example, mentions a teacher who described a colleague as 'brilliant [though] it's difficult to explain. Mrs Carter doesn't shout a lot, doesn't punish a lot, but she gets the most amazing work out of these kids. She's fantastic. She treats children exactly the way they ought to be treated – not harshly, not soft, just right.' However, while the complexities of teaching will always allow for a certain *je ne sais quoi* in the performance of front-rank experts, there is also, arguably, a certain amount of craft and technique in the art based on general principles that can be learned and which is open to analysis.

'I applaud attempts to sell science, but I don't really approve of staff wearing tee-shirts.'

1.8   Such principles would help to construct a theory that had general applicability. What then are the conditions for an adequate theory or model of teaching? I would say there are at least five essential ones:

(a) It must be comprehensive. Since so many aspects depend on each other, to omit any might distort the picture.

(b) At the same time it must not be so complex as to defy understanding. The purpose of a 'model' is to portray complexity in simpler terms. It must therefore be economical.

(c) Its terms, and the relationships between them must be clear, permitting of no ambiguity, inconsistency or misunderstanding.

(d) The theory, of necessity, must be tentative, since so little evidence exists about 'good' or 'effective' teaching that meets conditions (a)–(c), despite an enormous literature. As more evidence becomes available, the theory may need to be modified, but confidence in the theory increases.

(e) The theory must be available for testing by trial and error. There is little use in devising a theory that you have to either take or leave and cannot apply to other situations to see if the same properties and interconnections still hold.

1.9   With these conditions in mind, we can now look at some contrasting attempts to get to grips with the essence of teaching. I shall begin with the one that we might call an 'official' view of good teaching, as defined by the DES, Her Majesty's Inspectorate and OFSTED. It must be understood at the outset, of course, that these agencies are concerned with the efficiency of the system within the policy of the government of the day. This shows a real interest in the quality of teaching, but also a political concern for value for money. The DES is concerned to promote that policy. HM Inspectorate has more independence, but is still attached to the DES, and the efforts of the inspectors are largely directed towards making the system work. This is even more the case now the inspection of schools has been taken over by OFSTED (see the Fact Book, p. 65). We would therefore expect to find attention given to such matters as how schools might best organize themselves for effective teaching, what local education authorities might do to ensure appropriate conditions and to deploy the teaching force most effectively, and how training institutions can help produce 'good' teachers. I shall now examine the consequences of this.

2 THE 'GOOD' TEACHER – OFFICIAL

'You don't think you're in danger of taking the idea of "Living History" a little too far, Mr Winthrop?

'No, I've not learned anything today – we had to listen to the teacher all day … '

'If schools are bad, then they should be made to be good. If teachers can't teach, they shouldn't be teaching at all'
(Tony Blair, Labour Party Conference, October 1994.)

The teaching force, some 440,000 strong, is the major single determinant of the quality of education.
(DES, 1983, paragraph 1.)

'Academics have tried to identify the elusive qualities of good teachers. Thousands of studies have been undertaken … but with as much success as the quest for the philosopher's stone.'
(Wragg, 1991, p. vi.)

2.1   Government documents from the DES, such as *Teaching Quality* (1983), *Better Schools* (1985) and *Education Observed 3 – Good Teachers* (1985a), and more recent OFSTED publications (e.g. 1992, 1994) reflect the growing concern with the quality of teaching and the belief reflected in the second quotation above. This has to be seen within the prevailing political context. For example, some might argue that the first two quotations above are political statements rather than scientific judgements. We might come to a view about that if we examine the methods that underlie the conclusions given in the reports. At the same time we might be able to formulate a model of what is officially regarded as 'good' teaching (though this is never explicitly stated in these reports). A report by HM Inspectorate, *The New Teacher in School* (DES, 1982), provides a useful illustration of what we might call an 'official' view of good teaching. The aims of the inquiry were to 'assess how well newly trained teachers in general are equipped for the work they are assigned in their first posts' and to judge how far schools make best use of what new teachers have to offer. A hundred and thirty inspectors were involved, visiting 294 primary and secondary schools of various types for a day. They used questionnaires, held interviews and observed one probationer in each school for two lessons, observing 588 lessons in all.

Activity 3   (allow about 5 minutes) ─────────────────────

How adequate do you consider these methods for evaluating teachers? Think about matters like sampling, inter-observer reliability, balance of observation and other methods used. What methods would be necessary, in your opinion, to meet the aims of the inquiry?

My comments appear in the course of the following text.

───

2.2   The report caused quite a furore in the press when it appeared, for the inspectors reported that 'nearly a quarter of the teachers in the present sample [were] poorly or very poorly equipped for the task they are given to do'. This appears to be getting worse. In his 1995 annual report, the Chief Inspector for Schools said that between a third and a quarter of lessons in primary schools were unsatisfactory. Qualifications were made in the 1982 report. For example, the heads of the schools were rather more generous in their estimations of probationers' suitability and the inspectors themselves thought that where there were serious weaknesses in teaching they were in many cases made worse by the circumstances of the lessons. Some commentators (e.g. McNamara, 1986) thought more should have been made of these points. The inspectors also recognized that some teachers 'would undoubtedly improve substantially' and they noted possible limitations in the methods used (e.g. probationers observed for only two lessons; the problem of the effect on inexperienced teachers of being observed). Despite this, many took the report as evidence that there were serious problems with the quality of teaching in general.

Activity 4 (allow about 10 minutes) ——————————————————

Our concern here is to try to identify the criteria the inspectors used in reaching their judgement. The criteria, they say, are those they would use for 'assessing any work in schools' and are 'implicit in the evaluation of work seen' (DES, 1982, p. 3). I have reprinted extracts from the report on some model lessons. See if you can identify the criteria within them that would warrant their being considered excellent. What sort of picture of 'the model teacher' do they construct?

Primary schools

In primary schools such work fell into two distinct categories. In the first category were lessons where the teacher worked mainly with the class as a whole. Sometimes the work was the same for all but sometimes a common introduction led to differentiated work. In these lessons there appeared to be a well planned approach where the beginning aroused interest and all the children were drawn in. Development then led to the setting of tasks where either through some differentiation, or through teacher support and challenge, an attempt was made to cater for different abilities. The lessons ended with discussion which drew the work together and brought them to a satisfactory conclusion.

An English lesson for a 29-pupil class of 8-year-olds started with the children seated around the teacher in a carpeted area of a mobile classroom. The teacher played a tape-recording of a market trader selling a toy. The 'patter' gave a vague though colourful description of the toy with a warning of dire effects if the red and yellow buttons were pressed at the same time. The children's interest and curiosity were aroused and there were many questions during the discussion which followed. Sections of the tape were replayed when necessary in order that the pupils could work out their own answers. The children then wrote their own descriptions of the toy, describing what would happen if the buttons were pressed. The teacher moved around the class working with individuals and small groups of children, listening, questioning and extending responses.

Different kinds of classroom organization

Another example was a 26-pupil class of 10-year-olds following a long-term project on their immediate environment. A large-scale plan of a housing estate was available and the children discussed what should be provided – houses, schools, shops, street lighting, play areas – and where they should be placed. Through skilful questioning the children were made to think like planners and they began to explore the central ideas of people living together in close community. At one time two groups of children disagreed strongly about the siting of a school and were required to examine the evidence which they had produced. All the children were involved at all stages of the lesson.

An example of a lesson in which a common introduction led into differentiated work was one with a 31-pupil class of 9-year-olds in mathematics. The lesson began with a revision of work previously done on area and perimeter. Questioning was appropriately varied, challenging the more able pupils and encouraging the least able. Examples were demonstrated on the blackboard and two levels of follow-up work were provided. The pupils were encouraged to check their calculations by drawing diagrams on squared paper. The teacher worked with individual children; as they finished this work it was checked and they were given graded worksheets of a suitable level of difficulty.

The second type of lesson was that devoted mainly or entirely to group and/or individual work. Sometimes the children were working on the same subject, for example, in mathematics using commercially produced assignment cards, sometimes on more than one subject. Children knew what to do and moved easily and quietly into groups. The range of work was well supported by equipment. Activity was developed and sustained by the teacher's timely interventions. Where appropriate the lesson ended with a short class discussion.

Eight-year-old children were engaged on a lesson which involved group and individual work in more than one subject area. The class was divided into three groups and continued with work started on the previous day. The first group worked from commercial work cards, consulting with the teacher when necessary. A range of appropriate support material was available. In an adjoining work area, children were engaged on a series of experiments on floating and sinking. The work was well-structured, appropriate materials were at hand and pupils were encouraged to form hypotheses, observe carefully and make deductions. The third group of children had collected a variety of musical instruments and were using these to answer questions on prepared work cards. The questions sometimes called for specific answers (e.g. 'How can you play a high or a low note?') or more open ended responses (e.g. 'Describe the instrument or comment on the sounds it makes.').

Secondary schools

The aim of a laboratory lesson in biology with 23 low-ability second-year pupils was to extend recent work on reproduction. The lesson started with good questioning techniques, through the extension of pupils' language ('when the sperm goes into the egg' became 'when the sperm fertilizes the egg'), the teacher's own use of language (the pupils' 'stat' became 'thermostat') and exploitation of pupils' responses. A demonstration followed and fertilized hen's eggs at various stages of development were opened and examined by pupils. This produced considerable interest and many questions, all of which were handled in an encouraging and confident manner. One pupil asked how chicks breathe and the class was invited to scan their booklets, where they found the necessary information. Pupils were constantly encouraged to observe, speculate and look for patterns. Opportunities were provided for individual and small-group work and the teacher moved easily about the class questioning, reinforcing and, where appropriate, extending the explanation. Finally, pupils were asked to write their own account of how the egg was opened and what was observed with questions such as, 'Why should eggs be turned regularly during incubation?' and 'Why is the embryo near the top of the opened egg?' set for homework. The pupils were involved and interested and scientific thinking was encouraged.

In a history lesson, 30 able 11-year-olds had been engaged in examining various ways in which historians learn about the past – in particular about the Romans. Previous written work revealed an excellent range of topics and approaches involving diagrams, maps, imaginative writing and critical examination of different types of evidence. The lesson opened with a reminder of previous enquiries and a display of aerial photographs to illustrate how ancient buildings, field systems, etc., can be identified. This led through open-ended questioning to discussion of the role of the archaeologist and a comparison was drawn with the work of a detective. The exercise set for the pupils was the examination of a 'coin hoard' consisting of coins from 1860 to the present day. Pupils were asked to make deductions and this led to good oral work including extended responses. The question 'How do we explain the small quantity of foreign coins in a mainly British collection?' evoked spirited and ingenious replies. The lesson proceeded by means of short explanations by the teacher, coupled with searching questions. The objective was clear – a critical examination of historical evidence – and the pupils were closely involved in the activity.

(DES, 1982, paragraphs 2.52–2.59, pp. 20–22.)

'And that's old Ted Billington – none of your fancy projects for him – a couple of hours setting up, a few bangs, a bloody awful smell and bags of notes … '

2.3   From such lessons, and others like them, the inspectors built up a picture of successful lessons. They would involve good relationships between teachers and pupils, with the teacher showing:

… a quiet, calm, relaxed, good-humoured attitude … combined with firmness and a sense of purpose; a demonstration of interest in and knowledge of the pupils individually and an appropriate level of expectation of them; and mutual respect ... the teachers being sensitive to the needs of the pupils and respecting their contributions whatever their limitations. Where these qualities were shown, pupils were confident enough to play a full part in the lessons, to offer their own ideas and ask questions or seek help when unsure, while the teacher could blend praise and encouragement with an occasional reprimand, the latter without arousing resentment.

(DES, 1982, pp. 6–7.)

progressivist

2.4   Good classroom management is associated with 'a crisp, orderly, punctual start to the lesson ... a planned and tidy ending, an assured manner, good use of the eye and voice and the giving, where necessary, of clear instructions' (p. 7). In primary classrooms, where pupils may be working on a variety of tasks and subjects, 'the teachers should move purposefully around the classroom anticipating needs, checking and extending the pupils' work' (p. 7).

2.5   There should be appropriate aims and objectives, taking account of the age and abilities of the class, their previous experience and the nature of the subject being studied. Where aims were inappropriate, it was often because they were too limited, being based on 'the recording or memorizing of facts or the practice of techniques without any attempt to develop a depth of understanding or to maintain a progression' (p. 9). Pupils' work should be 'thoroughly and constructively marked'. Appropriate books, materials and equipment for the range of pupils present should be selected. Inspectors recognized, here, possible problems of resource in the school, but were concerned about 'lessons in which teachers had resigned themselves to using the inadequate or unsuitable materials available in their schools and had made no attempt to supplement or adapt them' (p. 10).

2.6   Work should be matched to pupils' capabilities and needs. In primary schools, lessons which did this 'called on a number of teaching techniques: assignments at different levels after a class exposition, well-differentiated work-cards, skilfully varied oral questioning which maintained a good pace and individual and group work with well organized intervention by the teacher' (p. 12). Older pupils did not become bored, nor the less able frustrated. Opportunities were provided for pupils to take 'increasing responsibility for organizing some parts of their own work', giving them 'a sense of purpose in their work', increasing motivation and developing 'self-reliance and co-operation' (p. 13). In secondary schools, such lessons showed 'a good choice of teaching materials which made demands on the pupils, well-planned purposeful tasks which allowed for contributions from pupils of different ability, good well-paced oral work with differentiated levels of questioning, and a variety of learning styles combining class exposition with group or individual work' (p. 14). Mastery of a subject is clearly very important. Without it, teaching approaches often maintained 'slavish adherence to the textbook, reliance on narrow questions often requiring monosyllabic answers, an inability to follow up and extend pupils' answers and an over-prescriptive method whereby the teacher was able to remain within a constricted, safe pattern of work' (pp. 14–15).

16

2.7   Language in the classroom was seen as an important area. There should be opportunities for useful dialogue between teachers and pupils, for pupils to express their own thoughts and ideas and to have their language extended. Teachers should vary their style of questioning to suit the occasion, and 'make good use of the pupils' responses to carry the work forward' (p. 18). In good lessons, questions were carefully balanced between those addressed to the whole class and those to named individuals. Some teachers 'were skilled at breaking down a problem into stages so that, by posing supplementary questions, they could narrow or broaden the scope of the inquiry helpfully for the pupils' (p. 19).

2.8   HM Inspectors point out that all these factors were 'clearly interdependent and it was rare to find work of high quality in respect of some but not of others'. This, perhaps, reinforces their point that 'the personal qualities of the teachers were in many cases the decisive factor in their effectiveness' (p. 80). Some, in their opinion, were clearly unsuited to teaching and the training institutions were taken to task for passing them as fitted for teaching.

Activity 5   (allow about 10 minutes) ────────────────────

Before going on, consider the following points:

(a) You might think that this is a model of good practice that most people would agree with and that it leaves little to argue about. It is, however, founded upon certain principles derived from a particular theory, or theories, of learning. See if you can identify some of these principles. They will be considered in Block 3 Unit 4.

(b) The inquiry leading up to the report occurred during a time of falling rolls in secondary schools and, in official estimation, a surplus of teachers. What difference do you think these facts and the kind of climate associated with them might have made to the conclusions reached that about 25 per cent of new teachers were inadequate and that the major causes of inadequacy were personal qualities? Compare the period following the Second World War, when there was a desperate shortage of teachers, many were 'emergency trained' and, for many years, graduates were regarded as qualified to teach without having had to undertake any specialist teacher training.

(c) By placing the emphasis on personal qualities, the inspectors are employing a deficit model: that is to say, they believe there is something within these teachers that is deficient. Can you think of any other possible explanations? Think of things external to those teachers, that may perhaps be outside their control.

'Just tell me ... at the end of your lessons, do they murmur "ineffective, ineffective"?'

2.9   It would be difficult to imagine such a conclusion in the 1940s or 1950s. When I first started teaching it was in a primary school as an untrained graduate. As a graduate, I was recognized as qualified and actually received more pay than non-graduates who had been trained and had had several years' experience. This was a gross injustice of which I was only too well aware. I was an amateur enjoying the culture of the school, but fumbling around, compared with professionals who knew what they were doing. This anomaly has, of course, since been rectified, but not before the demand for and supply of teachers warranted it. Standards of adequacy are almost inevitably affected by social and political climate. As for the 'deficit model', the inspectors do themselves refer from time to time in the report to 'other factors'. You might argue that these, and others not mentioned, need to be given greater prominence. Much of what the inspectors criticize in lessons in the report appears to be fairly common in schools – too much direction by teachers, failure to distinguish among pupils in mixed-ability classes, boring tasks, the dictating of notes, etc. If this is the case, one suspects that the scale of the inadequacy is almost certainly too vast to be put down solely to teachers' deficiency.

dependent on the Chn, school, community...

2.10   As for 'personal quality' being the decisive factor in effective teaching, McNamara (1986) has pointed out that there is no indication that this arose during the research as a key variable that required definition, close observation and analysis. 'The notion of "personal quality" is merely invoked … after the research has been completed in order to account for the so called findings' (p. 32). Further, it is not related to the extensive literature on teachers' personality, which shows the problems in relating it to effective teaching. For example, we might approve of qualities a teacher possesses, but that teacher may not be able to employ them in such a way as to help pupils to learn. You might be able to think of a number of other problems about the question of a teacher's personal qualities. (Is it possible for everyone to agree on whether a particular teacher has good personal qualities or not? Do all teachers require the same kind of qualities? Should not the teaching staff of a school reflect a variety of views, personalities, qualities, and so on?)

2.11   *The New Teacher in School* put the issue of 'quality' on the agenda, whatever the problems surrounding it, presented an outline model of the Inspectorate's conception of it and evaluated a number of teachers in terms of it. The emphasis on 'quality' and how to secure it has grown with further publications. If *The New Teacher in School* had its sights on training institutions, *Teaching Quality* (DES, 1983) was aimed at local education authorities, discussing how they could help to 'improve the match between teacher expertise and subjects taught' and 'raise professional standards by retaining and encouraging the best and most committed teachers … making full use of management tools such as premature retirement, redeployment and, if necessary, compulsory redundancy in the interests of achieving a good match between their teachers' qualifications and skills and the needs of teachers in the schools' (paragraph 8). *Better Schools* (DES, 1985) continued with the related quests to 'expose the heart of good teaching' (paragraph 135) and to manage the teaching force to ultimate efficiency, better teachers being promoted, those 'encountering professional difficulties' being identified and counselled and, where that did not work, being considered for 'early retirement or dismissal' (paragraph 180).

2.12   From these publications, Broadhead (1987) has extracted a wider model of presumed good practice. It is worth giving this in full. (The

18

references are to *The New Teacher in School* (NTS), *Education Observed 3 – Good Teachers* (EO) and *Better Schools* (BS).) As Broadhead points out, this is a prescriptive model listing qualities to which it is thought all teachers should aspire, though *in toto* they are recognized as probably being beyond the reach of any one teacher. They are an ideal to be aspired towards.

A blueprint for the good teacher?

The model
The professional behaviour

The good teacher is:

1   Reliable, punctual, co-operative and willing. EO5

2   Committed to further professional training. EO7/8

3   In conjunction with colleagues, able to establish long-term aims and short-term objectives and can set learning objectives. EO19

4   Capable of responding to professional teamwork. BS143

5   Capable of carrying out professional tasks without bias. BS144

6   Involved in after-school activities and clubs. EO29/32, NTS5.5

The personal characteristics

The good teacher is:

1   Enthusiastic, hard working, common sensical, firm, intelligent, adaptable, tenacious, intuitive, sensitive, friendly, energetic, conscientious, imaginative, resourceful. NTS3.3, NTS5.5

2   Able to command the respect of pupils and maintain excellent relations. EO6, NTS3.3

3   Able to control the class. EO13

4   Able to hold the pupils' interest. BS140

5   Able to make use of a repertoire of teaching styles. EO10, BS14

6   Capable of gaining access to a variety of teaching strategies. BS136/138, NTS3.3

7   Able to communicate lesson objectives to the pupils. EO19

8   Able to incorporate personal example into classroom life. EO3, BS19

9   Able to establish good relationships with parents and the community. EO34

10 Able to bring something new into the school and be a source of ideas. NTS5.5

11 Able to seek and receive advice. NTS5.5

12 Able to demonstrate a specialist, in-depth knowledge in one subject and a wide range of general subject expertise. NTS5.5

The organized attributes

The good teacher is:

1   Able to engage in long- and short-term lesson planning. EO19, NTS3.3

2   Able to gain access to teaching aids/resources for both self and pupils. EO20

3   Proficient in class management and the grouping of pupils. BS138

4   Able to make available a diversity of subject matter with the classroom. EO13

5   Able to select and present subject matter that will engage the pupils' interest. BS133

6   Able to encourage pupil exploration by linguistic means by careful and sensitive questioning and the development of small group activities. EO17

7   Able to encourage the development of pupils' listening skills. EO17

8   Able to communicate the assessment of performance to individual pupils. EO21/27

The perceptive qualities

The good teacher is:

1   Able to undertake the role of guide and mentor to pupils when required. BS135

2   Able to perceive and respond to individual pupil differences. EO11, NTS3.3

3   Able to determine external factors which are affecting individual pupils. EO19

4   Able to modify own language and explanation to pupils' needs when so required. EO11

5   Able to perceive and respond to an external event or sudden upsurge of interest exhibited by the pupils and incorporate this into daily lesson planning. EO19

6   Able to evaluate the effectiveness of his/her own teaching methods. BS134

7   Able to evaluate the relevance of the subject material. BS45, NTS3.3/5.5

The information-gathering skills and evaluative skills

The good teacher is:

1   Proficient at gathering information pertaining to individual pupils' progress. EO24

2   Proficient at identifying reasons for failure. BS110

3   Aware of temporary/permanent factors which may be affecting pupils' behaviour/learning skills. BS139, EO7

4   Skilful at drawing on individual pupils' experience. BS137

5   Capable of developing access to knowledge of which subject matters will engage the pupils' interest. BS139, NTS3.3

6   Aware of the categories of information that pupils need access to. BS133

7   Thorough in his/her marking. NTS5.5

8   Aware of the teaching aids and resources that are required in a general classroom sense and regarding a specific lesson based need. EO24

(Broadhead, 1987, pp. 64–66.)

Activity 6   (allow about 15 minutes) ───────────────────────────

Few perhaps would quarrel with many of these attributes – they make a useful compilation for any professional job connected with people, but consider these questions:

(a) What is the purpose of this 'blueprint'? If it is intended to explain the part played by the teacher in effective learning, how adequate is it? What else would need to be considered?

(b) A good test of the usefulness of a model is its approximation to reality. How close to the realities of classroom life is this one?

(c) HM Inspectors categorize teachers in these reports ('good', 'poor', 'very poor', etc). They obviously find it useful to do so, but could such a strategy have drawbacks in a teacher's professional development?

───

2.13   Some might argue that these reports should be seen within the context of growing central control of the educational system. The criteria are centrally determined rating systems (as opposed, for example, to being determined by the teachers themselves), set up to measure teachers. The reports contain strong suggestions about how the criteria can be met, but this must be done within the prevailing system and with existing resources. Interestingly, *The New Teacher in School* carries a disclaimer inside its front cover to the effect that: 'Nothing said in this discussion paper is to be construed as implying Government commitment to the provision of additional resources.' As for the system, DES Circular 3/84 stated: 'In assessing the personal qualities of candidates, institutions should look in particular for a sense of responsibility, a robust but balanced outlook, awareness, sensitivity, enthusiasm and facility in communication' (paragraph 14). As McNamara (1986, p. 36) points out, an educational argument could easily be advanced for replacing what might be seen as the conservative 'robust but balanced' with the radical 'critical and reformist'.

Effective teachers are good at … ?

2.14   As for an explanation of teacher effectiveness, Broadhead feels that not enough consideration has been given to factors that impinge on 'all teachers' work which lie outside their control' (DES, 1985a, paragraph 3). This would include those I discussed before, but Broadhead points particularly to the enormous disparity between children of different age groups, their different needs and, consequently, different demands from teachers. Yet even though the inspectors occasionally draw a distinction between primary and secondary teachers, the assumption seems to be that one model, by and large, fits all. They have missed, too, Broadhead argues, the complexities of relationships within the classroom. 'Real life' has been reduced to a 'plethora of prescriptive descriptions' (Broadhead, 1987, p. 68).

Not taking into account individual situations.

2.15   What we have, then, is not a theory of successful teaching, but a checklist of points that might be useful in appraisal of a teacher by somebody who is observing the teacher. The list does not contain guidance on how a teacher might improve his or her personal effectiveness beyond the implication that 'weeding-out' and behaviour modification will enhance effectiveness. There is no consideration of what lies behind the teacher's behaviour. If behaviour is 'inadequate', it is considered to be redeemable at source and, if not, to be dispensed with. This reflects, perhaps, the new managerial ethos that pervades the environment in which the quality of teachers was being discussed.

2.16   There is also a problem in placing teachers in categories. It might be a useful 'sorting' device, but in terms of professional development it might prove counter-productive. A lesson might be drawn here from the literature pointing to the dangers of labelling pupils. We may shape our behaviour towards pupils in accordance with the labels we put on them and they may come to respond in line with that: that is, they come to act out and, hence, confirm the behaviour we expect of them. Broadhead concludes that 'perhaps the issues to which those concerned with developing a theory of educational effectiveness should be addressing themselves are not "What is the ideal state and how many have made it?", but "What is happening along the way?"' (Broadhead, 1987, p. 70).

2.17   Research is available here in areas such as teaching styles and classroom tasks, as mentioned earlier (para. 1.2), and these do show the problems of getting to grips with the complexities of teaching. The 'teaching styles' approach followed the line of development established by the Plowden report (CACE, 1967) in terms of 'traditional' and 'progressive' styles of teaching, but it has become clear that there are problems in classifying teachers in this way. Differences within teaching styles appeared greater than those between styles, but in any event the results were not conclusive. The research on the quality of pupils' learning experiences (Bennett *et al.*, 1984) broke new ground and raised important points about how far the tasks that pupils were asked to perform 'matched' their abilities. We may, however, query whether teaching and learning can be reduced to a series of tasks; and teachers' and pupils' subjectivities and motivation were left out of account, as were social factors and constraints surrounding the tasks. An equally important question, therefore, is 'What are the conditions that affect teaching efficiency?' which I consider in

Sections 3 and 4. This will lead to a somewhat different model of 'good teaching'.

Activity 7 (allow about 10 minutes) ————————————————————

Now refer back to the conditions specified for an adequate theory in paragraph 1.8. Consider each point and say how far you think the documents discussed in this section and the model outlined by Broadhead meet those conditions.

Comment ————————————————————————————————

(a) *Comprehensive* There is recognition (a) that many of these aspects of personal quality hang together and (b) of 'other factors'. For example, *The New Teacher in School* took note of 'constraints' that appeared to be affecting the lessons that were observed, taking into account such matters as the reported 'difficulty' of a class or group, 'the availability of suitable materials or equipment … '. These 'constraints' were all 'within-school' constraints and amenable to treatment by individual schools.

No account was taken of differences between schools. Some would argue that you cannot separate teachers from their schools in this way, so much depends on school policy, ethos, management structure, neighbourhood, etc. (see Block 3 Unit 6). Nor is any account taken of the general system within which schools and teachers operate. I shall say more about this in Section 5, but it should be clear that the theory or model implicit in these reports is not very comprehensive.

(b) *Economical* The model as derived by Broadhead seems rather diffuse.

(c) *Clarity* Here I confess to the same sort of difficulty outlined in paragraph 1.5. Looking at the model described in paragraph 2.12, I find that many of the qualities listed are vague and begging of further questions. In the first section, for example, on 'professional behaviour', I wonder what 'reliable', 'co-operative' and 'willing' mean? Who defines these and decides whether a teacher matches up to them? 'Co-operative' in what? 'Willing' to do what? Who are to be the arbiters of what counts as 'bias'? Would you expect 'good teachers' today to be involved in voluntary after school activities? It will be seen that none of these items are independent of political considerations. The first item in the second section (on 'personal characteristics') raises other doubts. You have seen some of the problems with 'common sense' and 'intuition'. How do these other qualities translate into practice? Are they not rather vacuous as they stand, transferable to almost any area of citizenship, or even a master criminal?

(d) *Tentative* The model is not at all tentative. The qualities of 'good teaching' are known in advance of the investigation.

(e) *Amenable to test* Parts of the model extracted by Broadhead might be amenable to test, though with a great deal of redefinition. In general, nothing is stated in that form or with that in view. In the light of point (d) above, it is not considered necessary.

We must conclude, therefore, that these reports have their shortcomings if you are seeking a theory of good teaching within them. Perhaps if HM Inspectorate had chosen to be more explicit about this, it might have produced something more adequate than the model compiled by Broadhead. As matters stand, the version coming through in the reports does not appear to be well grounded scientifically.

In fairness to the inspectors, they have, in some reports, given greater prominence to the conditions in which teachers work (see point (a) above): for example, in their reports on the effects of the expenditure policies of local education authorities on educational provision in England. One report (DES, 1986, p. 11) argues that for high quality teaching to be sustained and increased ' ... there is a need for the resources necessary to do the job well; decent, stimulating conditions in which to work; and that respect and support which are the mirror images of professional commitment and competence'. Unfortunately, and perhaps significantly, these reports do not receive the same amount of publicity and influence as those discussed in Section 2.

support individual circumstances.

Reading   (allow about 1 hour) ————————————

Since the reports discussed here were published, there have been major developments in education, including the Education Reform Act of 1988 (see the Fact Book, p. 61) and the establishment of the Office for Standards in Education (OFSTED) in 1992 (see the Fact Book, p. 65). OFSTED is likely to exert considerable influence on teaching, with its target of inspecting all schools every four years. *The Handbook for the Inspection of Schools* (OFSTED, 1992) sets the parameters for the inspection. Other key documents have been *Primary Matters* (OFSTED, 1994) and the DES Discussion Paper *Curriculum Organisation and Classroom Practice* (Alexander *et al.*, 1992). To what extent do these confirm or extend the 'official' model of the 'good teacher' of the 1980s? To what extent do they construct a different model? How do you account for the changes? Consider these questions, and write brief notes in answer to them, as you read Troman 'Models of the good teacher: defining and redefining teacher quality', in Reader 2 (Woods).

3   TEACHERS' VALUES, INTERESTS AND MOTIVATION

3.1   So far I have discussed teaching as if what teaching means can be taken for granted and as if teaching is what all teachers wish equally to do. Also, teaching has been considered as if teachers are free to decide how to go about their classroom practice; in other words, as if 'teaching' has been studied as a technical process employed by teachers for effective learning. Teaching, however, is a highly personal process. You have to feel motivated to teach and feelings enter strongly into a teacher's sense of accomplishment. Teachers also differ in their approach to teaching. They may have different interests and different levels of commitment. I now want to examine these two aspects of teaching and to consider the implications for learning outcomes.

Feelings enter strongly into a teacher's sense of accomplishment

TEACHERS' COMMITMENT

3.2   It is often argued that one of the most important factors in successful teaching is pupils' motivation (this is to be considered in the following unit). Less attention has been paid to *teachers'* motivation, which tends to be taken for granted. Not all teachers, however, are equally committed to teaching or in the same way (Lacey, 1977). Some are thoroughly dedicated, others less so. Some of the former teach because they love to do so and love children (what might be termed 'vocational commitment'); some *progressivist* because they consider it a good professional job in which they can excel and advance (what might be termed 'professional commitment'). Some *traditionalist* might be in teaching for what they can get out of it materially ('instrumental commitment'). Some might be keen to promote a cause ('political commitment'). The concept of commitment has become topical in recent years when there has been a crisis of morale throughout the profession and some teachers have been found to re-examine their involvement with the job. It must inevitably affect teaching efficiency, especially as it seems that the 'caring' teacher has been one of those most at risk (Vernon, 1986).

instrumental (handwritten, left margin)

3.3 Sikes *et al.* have summarized the various studies of commitment as follows:

> … we have put together analyses from other recent work on this (Lacey, 1977; Woods, 1979; Nias, 1981), with our own indications from this study to provide a composite model.

Forms of teacher commitment

	Vocational		Professional		Instrumental
	Education	Subject	Teaching	Institution	Career
Core					
Mixed					
Peripheral					

> This shows a vocational 'calling' to teach or dedication to a set of ideals about education; a professional commitment to subject-based teaching, to teaching as an art or craft, and to the institution, such as the school; and an instrumental commitment to a teacher career purely as a useful career to be in. An individual teacher may show one, some, or all, of these types, may vary them from time to time, or at certain ages … and may also vary in intensity of commitment from core to peripheral. We might hypothesize that the teacher career generally sees a shift from left to right [of the figure] as it progresses, with a corresponding switch between core and peripheral. The initial phase of the teacher's career in our sample marks a progression from vocational to professional commitment, and it is not unreasonable to assume an increase in instrumental commitment during the 'settling down' phase of the life cycle, when many teachers acquire or extend their familiar responsibilities. But shifts may be more fluid than this, depending on certain critical incidents. These need not necessarily all be in the same direction. A good crop of examination results, an unexpected piece of good work from a particular child, a generous pay award, an increase in in-service provision, a lowering of the teacher–pupil ratio – such events might induce a shift from right to left. Others – for example, a bad experience with some disruptive pupils, an unsatisfactory pay award, a piece of educational policy of which they disapproved, being 'passed over' for promotion – may promote a shift to the right.
>
> During the current critical period, with the profession under contraction, the schools under-resourced by comparison with the 1970s and deep dissatisfaction about salary levels, we might expect a left–right, and a top–bottom shift, or a combination of the two. This might be accompanied by the development of alternative careers outside teaching, in some other occupation or business, in the family, or in a hobby.

(Sikes *et al.*, 1985, pp. 237–38.)

[handwritten margin note: teaching style can change depending on age, subject, theme...]

Most teachers have a strong sense of values

3.4   This illustrates some possible variability in commitment depending on the matching of a person to the job. It points to possible changes in the view people have of themselves over a period of time and to the influence on teaching of other factors that have serious implications for the teacher and, consequently, for the quality of his or her work.

TEACHERS' VALUES AND INTERESTS

3.5   Most teachers have a strong sense of values. They teach because they believe in something, and they want to see it conveyed. They have a conception of the 'good life', and the 'good citizen'. They know what kind of society they would like, what kind of personal and social values they wish to encourage, what knowledge they wish to convey, and how. All these things are interconnected. Teaching is, at heart, a moral craft (Tom, 1988; Elbaz, 1992). Teachers put a large part of their 'selves' into their teaching. Nias describes the trouble some (primary) teachers go to in order to find the right niche for their 'selves':

reconstruction/ instrumental

> Once individuals felt technically confident, their willingness to identify as 'teachers' depended in large measure on their ability to find a school or sector of education which 'felt right for me', which would enable them to 'be myself'. They began to change jobs, 'looking for a school where I'd feel I fitted in' – several moved three or four times in as many years. All of them trained for work in primary or middle schools, yet within their first decade of work, one or another of them had taught in fifteen different types of school, other than mainstream state schools for children of 5–13 years. Between them they found 'the right place for me': in further education; remedial and subject departments in secondary schools; private, denominational, nursery, hospital, and special schools (of five different sorts); and home teaching. They also tried working in schools with large numbers of Asian, Caribbean, Italian or 'traveller' children, and in inner-city, suburban, and rural areas. So, the teacher (one of seven to move to special schools) who applied for a job in a hospital school said, 'As a teacher in an ordinary job, I cannot give children the attention I feel they need. With smaller numbers I can care more, and that's what I want to do'; and the infant teacher who moved to the remedial department of a secondary school explained, 'I knew that in that department, children came first, as I believe they should'. Similarly, two teachers had deliberately changed from schools on re-settlement estates to suburban areas, because, as one said, 'I don't believe that teachers should be social workers, I want to *teach*'. Others moved for similar reasons, one commenting that they could not 'use [their] art in that school', another that 'there was no scope for [their] sort of English teaching'. In short, most of my interviewees were reluctant to give up teaching until they had satisfied themselves, through a careful search, that they could not 'be themselves' anywhere in the profession.
>
> (Nias, 1989, pp. 68–69.)

'finding your place'.

3.6   Once in the niche, they seek to protect and extend their selves through building alliances with like-minded others in 'reference sets'. A collaborative culture might develop – a 'set of norms about ways of behaving, perceiving and understanding underpinned by jointly held beliefs and values' (Nias *et al.*, 1992, p. 2). If they find themselves misplaced in a school, or otherwise deprived of avenues through which to operationalize their values, they might find themselves experiencing a form of bereavement, 'grieving for a lost self' (Nias, 1991).

3.7   Teachers by no means all agree on values, even within the same school. Mac an Ghaill (1992), for example, claimed a three-way division among the staff of a comprehensive school he studied into what he terms the 'professionals', the 'old collectivists' and the 'new entrepreneurs'.

The 'Professionals' — classical humanistic

Member of professional association, opposed to trade unions, supported the hierarchical structure of school administration and organization of the curriculum in terms of streaming, subject based, common-sense approach to learning, in favour of the norm referenced assessment, opposed to progressive educational theories and methods, adopted an authoritarian approach to students and an assimilationist perspective to black students, strong sense of loyalty to colleagues, overtly opposed to recent curricular initiatives …

They tended to be older members of staff and former grammar school teachers. Their authority and main influence stemmed from their position as senior management and as departmental heads of science, mathematics and languages.

The 'Old Collectivists' — progressivist

Usually a member of a trade union and active in past industrial action, often member of Labour Party, strongly opposed to Education Reform Act and changes in pay and conditions, highly critical of creation of extra supervisory positions in teaching, strong sense of 'us' and 'them' in relations with head-teacher, theoretically based student-centred pedagogy, supported comprehensive education and pastoral care system, in favour of criteria referenced assessment, adopted a multicultural/anti-racist and anti-sexist approach as part of equal opportunities for black students and girls, strongly supportive of colleagues, promoted values of collectivism, egalitarianism and meritocracy, opposed to vocationalism, ambivalent to recent curricular innovation but strongly opposed to its philosophical base …

The term refers not to their age but their fading ideological significance within the school. Their power within the school was based on their positions as heads of special needs, careers and English and senior positions in pastoral care and community links.

The 'New Entrepreneurs'

Member of teacher association emphasizing professional status of career, opposed to trade unions and industrial action, in favour of non-strike contract agreement, supportive of increased management responsibilities and classroom teachers' accountability and appraisal, adopted a pragmatic pedagogical approach with eclectic selection of ideas and practices from the Professionals and the Old Collectivists, strong commitment to expanding own departments/faculties and promotion of new courses, supporter of enterprise culture, emphasized importance of public relations in presentation and marketing of schooling as a commodity, implemented modern education technology, overtly ambitious with a strong commitment to career advancement, projected high self-profile within school, saw students as clients, adopted an assimilationist approach to black students but used language of multiculturalism and equal opportunities for girls, highly visible supporter of curricular initiatives, including vocationalism ...

They included five teachers who qualified during the last decade and who were highly influential within this group. Their power was based on their positions as faculty heads and as departmental heads of vocationally oriented subjects, including business studies, computer studies and vocational courses.

(Mac an Ghaill, 1992, pp. 179–80.)

3.8   Mac an Ghaill's analysis was based on teacher reactions to the 1988 Education Reform Act. We could take any major issue and there would almost certainly be a variety of responses depending on teacher values, rather than any one objective assessment.

Activity 8   (allow about 10 minutes) ———————————————————

The studies in this section are primarily 'ethnographic'. This method involves long-term research of a particular group, using mainly naturalistic observation and unstructured interviewing. On the details given, what would you consider to be (a) the strengths, (b) the limitations of these studies? How do they rate against the theoretical elements mentioned in paragraph 1.8?

Comment ————————————————————————————

Ethnography is typically strong on internal validity, using a battery of methods (observations, participation, interviews, documents) over a long period to build up a faithful representation of the perspectives of the people in the situation under study. In the course of time, thematic patterns might be observed in the accumulating material, with interconnections between various aspects. These would be investigated more fully and the theme or concept developed. Thus a kind of underlying knowledge is, on analysis, made explicit.

Ethnographers do not usually make strong claims that their results are generally applicable and so we do not know to how many teachers, or groups of teachers, Mac an Ghaill's analysis, for example, applies. We do not know if there are differences among men and women teachers, teachers at different levels of school, at different career junctures, of different training, working in different authorities, and so on. There is also a tendency to put people into categories, and to lose sight of how some categories may be combined in individuals. In some respects, selves are multi-dimensional rather than singular.

As for its relationship to the theoretical elements in paragraph 1.8, the categories appear to me to be clear, discrete and well founded in the empirical material, of which only a very small part is given in the unit. The model of teachers' interests is testable in the sense that related case studies could be set up in other schools (and among the different groups of teachers mentioned above). Ethnographers, however, are usually more interested in understanding the situation under study than in generalization and verification. The nature of the approach calls for intensive, qualitative work along a very restricted front. The findings in this section, therefore, have to be seen in this light.

3.9   Consideration of teachers' values, interests and commitment provides another dimension to the issue of the quality of teachers. As one teacher told Riseborough (1981), following a forced demotion after a school merger, 'You know, if you take this [status] away, not all the money in the world will make him feel content with his job, and this is what teaching is all about. You've got to feel right.' If you do not 'feel right', for whatever reason (demotion, depressed salary, troublesome, oppositional head or colleagues, disruptive pupils, crowded timetable, problematic home life), it matters little, I suspect, whether you are 'traditionalist' or 'progressive' or what teaching style you were employing. The implications for policy are possibly to shift the burden of responsibility for good teaching, in part, from the teachers to the circumstances that bear on them. Teachers themselves are clearly a major determinant of the quality of work that they do, but if they 'do not feel right' because of factors beyond their control, such factors (school, LEA, or government policy) may bear a heavier responsibility. A different conclusion is therefore possible from that conveyed in the quotation from the DES at the beginning of Section 2. This will be further elaborated in the next section.

---

4   CONSTRAINTS ON TEACHERS

4.1   As well as influences such as commitment, values and interests bearing on teachers from within themselves, as it were, there are forces from without, over which the teacher may have little control. These are termed 'constraints' here because they delimit a teacher's field of activity. However, what might be a constraint for one teacher might be a creative opportunity for another. You have only to consider the differences in values and beliefs among the teachers identified in the extract from Sikes *et al.* in paragraph 3.3 to appreciate this. But whatever their positions, all teachers experience constraints of some kind or another, to some degree or other. Constraints do not stand apart from the teacher, but rather the two interact. Thus teachers might try to do something about the constraints, either by removing or modifying them, or by removing themselves to another situation, or by adapting their 'selves'. An example of one such adaptation was given in the discussion of commitment in paragraph 3.3. There are two broad kinds of constraint, those deriving from inside the school and those from the wider society outside the school, though the two are often interconnected.

SOCIETAL CONSTRAINTS

4.2   In recent years, teaching has been dominated by the demands of the National Curriculum and by other changes made by the 1988 Education Reform Act and subsequent ministerial orders (see Chapters 4 and 10 of the Fact Book). These changes have been represented as the product of world-wide developments, notably, in one influential approach, through the process of 'intensification' (Apple, 1986). The argument is that as advanced capitalist economies seek to maintain and promote efficiency, so the sphere of work narrows, high level tasks become routinized and there is more subservience to the bureaucratic whole. At the chalk-face there is more for teachers to do, including a proliferation of administrative and assessment tasks. There is less time to do it in, less time for re-skilling and for leisure and sociability, and few opportunities for creative work. There is a diversification of responsibility, notably with a high level of specification and direction, and a separation of conceptualization in long-term planning and policy-making (others) and of execution (teachers). There is a reduction in quality of service as corners are cut to cover the ground. The economic depression of the late 1980s and early 1990s brought on crises of accumulation and legitimation which gave an emphatic boost to these developments (Apple, 1988). Technical control processes impinged further upon the curriculum. Centralization, standardization and rationalization became the norm in policy circles. By 1992, there were some areas in the USA where 'it has been mandated that teachers must teach *only* that material which is in the approved text book' (Apple and Jungck, 1992, p. 20).

4.3   It is not difficult to find evidence from research done on the effects of the National Curriculum (introduced in 1988) in English primary schools to support the intensification thesis. What for some was 'a dream at conception' turned into a 'nightmare at delivery' (Campbell, 1993). It is clear that there was massive work overload, a loss of spontaneity and an increase in stress, that the sense of 'fun' and caring human relationships receded in some classrooms, that quantification replaced qualitative evaluation, that bureaucracy burgeoned, that some teachers felt that they had lost autonomy and control in the curriculum, that accountability became a matter of threat. Teachers feared further intrusion into pedagogy (see, for example, Drummond, 1991). Some argued that the way teachers think and feel had also been exploited. They had been caught in the 'trap of conscientiousness' (Campbell *et al.*, 1991), doing their best to meet the prescribed targets but compromising the quality of learning and their own health. Their inability to meet them all aggravates the 'guilt syndrome' (Hargreaves, 1994). If they do manage to meet them and celebrate their accomplishment, this may only be 'misrecognized professionalism' (Densmore, 1987). That is to say that teachers may feel more professional through mastering the range of technical criteria and tests accompanying the changes, whereas in reality this skill is yet another example of 'the administrative colonization' of teachers' time and space (Hargreaves, 1994, p. 109).

4.4   However, this is only one side of the picture. Pollard (1992) concluded that, in general, teachers in primary schools accepted the broad terms of the National Curriculum, and were seeking to implement it. The most striking feature of teachers' responses was their acceptance of it. Campbell *et al.* (1991b), in their study of infant teachers, observed that, though there were more serious sources of dissatisfaction, 'our evidence suggests that the imposed change of the National Curriculum, far from de-skilling and de-professionalizing the teachers, was, on the contrary, seen by them as extending their skills and increasing their professionalism' (p. 7). Campbell *et al.* (1991a, p. 31) concluded that primary school teachers' hearts and minds had been won over to the principle of the National Curriculum, and that the main issue was now one of manageability.

4.5   Manageability, however, was a huge problem, undermining potential support, raising a large number of specific concerns, such as oppressive workloads, increased bureaucracy, the pace of change, and uncertainty about how long a change would last before being modified. There were issues of spontaneity, autonomy, enjoyment, pupil–teacher relations, and stress. The new system of assessment was a major problem. In short, the pressures of implementation were in danger of expunging the potentially creative and liberating principles. These findings have been broadly reflected in the PACE research (Primary Assessment, Curriculum and Experience) covering both infant and junior schools (key stage 1 and key stage 2 in National Curriculum parlance). For example, Osborn *et al.* (1994) found that, though about 20 per cent of teachers actually felt empowered by the changes, for the majority of teachers, the impact of the changes on their work and role was perceived to be mostly negative, and that by 1993 a growing number of teachers were beginning to feel de-skilled. Many of them 'talked of a loss of freedom and creativity in their teaching, of feeling increasingly like "a machine for delivering a prescribed curriculum", as well as the loss of a career structure, and of doing a valued and worthwhile job' (p. 4).

4.6   The changes have resulted also in a plethora of curriculum initiatives at secondary school. The effects in one school are described as follows:

> What became clear as the research on the students progressed was that the management's and the teachers' bureaucratic over-concern

with the technical and administrative aspects of the curricular initiatives had resulted in their collective failure to acknowledge ... the centrality of meaning to educational change. More specifically, they failed to acknowledge the need to build shared meanings of the current innovations among and between the staff and students. This failure could not be explained simply in terms of individual teacher deficiencies. As some of the teachers pointed out, with the current restructuring of school organization, curriculum and assessment systems, institutions are increasingly under pressure to adopt reductionist models of education; in which schools are assumed to have no intrinsic value (use-value) but rather are seen as commodities that realize their value in the market place (exchange value) ... These teachers suggested that the introduction of the plethora of curricular initiatives could be understood as a means of increasing the school's productivity. Hence, this ensured their survival in the market place: 'putting bums on seats'. It was these changing material conditions which served to increase the ascribed high status of quantitative criteria in determining the design, implementation and evaluation of curriculum change. The emphasis was on the measurement of the product and the effectiveness and efficiency of its implementation rather than understanding the essential complexity and inter-subjectivity of the process of learning and teaching.

(Mac an Ghaill, 1992a, p. 223.)

'Sir, it has taken mankind thousands of years to get to Einstein; and you expect me to get there in three 45-minute lessons?'

4.7   These are examples of how international developments and government policies affect teaching in schools. There are other problems teachers have to contend with, notably the contradictory aim of educating all children to their maximum potential, but selecting and socializing them

36

Pressure to 'prepare' chn...

for society. Material constraints affect teaching aspirations. The level of funding determines the number of teachers employed, the kind and state of school buildings, the provision of books and other teaching aids, the amount of in-service training. Government policy fixes the pupils' length of schooling, the length of the school day and year, the number of teachers, terms and conditions of service, and general policy about kinds of schools (tripartite, comprehensive, grant maintained …) and curriculum. Thus matters like the pupil–teacher ratio, the teacher's timetable, and the contexts and aids for teaching are largely determined by forces external to the school.

4.8   Teachers are also subject to ideological influences. For example, from time to time educational ideologies appear which come to be defined as 'correct practice', and upon which career advancement depends. One such ideology – rather ironically, since it purports to be libertarian – is child-centred progressivism, which has been so influential in primary schools over the past thirty years, but which has come under attack recently. Alexander (1992, p. 169) noted the strength and influence of this ideology in the Leeds primary schools of his research. He observed that 'properly to belong one needed to accept and enact the ideology, and that mechanisms existed to encourage such acceptance'. By the late 1980s, it was, he argued, 'an ideology grounded in the best of intentions which for many has lost its early intellectual excitement and has become a mere shell of slogans and procedures, sometimes adopted for no other reason than the desire or need to conform' (Alexander, 1992, p. 194). It had bred a range of 'sacred cows and shibboleths' (such as 'enquiry methods', integration, resistance to subjects), and slogans, such as 'we teach children, not subjects', 'learning how to learn, rather than what to learn', 'discovery, not instruction'.

4.9   By the same token, the opposing ideology, that of 'traditionalism', also needs interrogating. In the early 1990s there was much talk among government ministers of 'back to basics' and traditional methods, and that this was only a matter of 'common sense'. As Alexander (1992, p. 194) notes, however, 'often as not, "common sense" means "my sense", my way of looking at the world, my values, my politics – and my power to impose them'.

School classrooms, buildings and grounds are important factors

4.10   The demands of society are mediated through the school. You will be studying the influence of the school in detail in Block 3, especially Unit 6, so I shall restrict discussion here to the main features. Prominent among them is the notion of the school 'ethos'. As yet, this is an ill-defined concept, but nonetheless one considered crucial to the effectiveness of a school (Rutter *et al.*, 1979). The ethos is manifested in things like the system of rewards and punishments, the nature of the relationships between teachers and pupils, the nature of pupils' participation in the school, the relative emphasis on academic or pastoral goals, the prevailing pedagogical orientation, the decision-making processes among the staff.

4.11   Rutter *et al.* found that schools with better behaviour and academic performance tended to have more teaching time (as opposed to other activities), planned their teaching on a group basis and had teachers who taught more than one subject. In lessons, teachers in such schools spent more time on the subject matter and less time on setting up equipment or handing out materials. They also included periods of quiet work in their lessons and started and finished lessons promptly. There was better behaviour where schools were neat and tidy, where there was more teacher continuity and adequate clerical help, and where children remained in the same group. It was, however, the *combined* effect of such variables that was much more powerful than any single item. This supports the views of such as Lawton (1987, p. 4), who argue that individual teachers are important, but limited in their effects, and that the question of the quality of teaching should also be seen in terms of the whole school.

traditionalist view.

4.12   The ethos may be informed by a particular educational philosophy and promoted by the headteacher through judicious appointments to staff as well as by direction of everyday activity, but schools are also affected by material and social factors, which might influence the view of possible and desirable goals. For example, schools that are situated in deprived inner-city areas with poor housing and high levels of unemployment may feel forced to elevate pastoral care and classroom control to the top priority over academic instruction. Such schools can become imbued with what Denscombe calls a 'low-achievement orientation':

> [This] results from mutually reinforcing expectations held by teachers and pupils where teachers, looking at factors like the social class, ethnic mix and material environment of the school, come to hold low expectations about the pupils' academic performance, while the pupils, reflecting such expectations and bringing relatively low academic aspirations from their social background, combine to produce a school ethos in which academic attainment gets written off as irrelevant.
>
> (Denscombe, 1985, p. 59.)

'Effective teaching' in such a context may amount to 'keeping 'em quiet'. In his research in three London comprehensive schools, Denscombe (1980)

39

actually found that the status of a teacher was judged by colleagues by the amount of noise issuing from a classroom and the number of times he or she referred difficult pupils to another teacher. This orientation, Denscombe argues, is aided by the organization of our schools into 'closed' classrooms. This all helps to promote 'a hidden pedagogy': that is, a tacit set of assumptions based on managing constraints rather than on principles of teaching.

Has their school a 'low achievement orientation'?

4.13   The notion of 'ethos' may also assume a degree of consensus within the school. This may be true of some schools, but others are more marked by conflict and a diversity of goals. Schools are divided into separate units (subject departments, year groups, houses, special groups) that develop their own agendas and loyalties, and may frequently come into conflict with each other. Such conflict may be about the provision of resources, status (particularly the status of one's subject) or about ideology. The latter is particularly salient for notions of 'effective teaching'. Sharp and Green have defined a teaching ideology as:

> *traditionalist*
>
> A connected set of systematically related beliefs and ideas about what are felt to be the essential features of teaching. A teaching ideology involves both cognitive and evaluative aspects, it will include general ideas and assumptions about the nature of knowledge and of human — *progressivist* nature – the latter entailing beliefs about motivation, learning and educability. It will include some characterization of society and the role and functions of education in the wider social context.
>
> (Sharp and Green, 1975 p. 68.)
>
> *instrumental / reconstructionist*

'Progressivism' is one such ideology, as is 'vocationalism' (see Block 6). Teachers within the same department might have profound differences on this score. In consequence, Ball (1987) has gone so far as to describe schools as 'arenas of struggle … riven with actual or potential conflict between members … poorly co-ordinated … ideologically diverse'.

4.14 It will be seen that studying isolated and discrete activities of teachers and pupils in the classroom has limited uses, for such activities gather meaning only from the historical, political, social, institutional and personal contexts within which they take place. A knowledge of such contexts would appear necessary for views of what is both possible and desirable teaching activity.

Reading (allow about 1 hour) ——————————————————

In effect, teachers are neither totally constrained, nor totally free to do what they want. Teachers' activity is invariably negotiated. There is always some degree of manoeuvre in the *implementation* of policy (Ball and Bowe, 1992). You should now read Woods and Jeffrey 'A new professional discourse? Adjusting to managerialism' in Reader 2 (Woods).

This article considers how some primary teachers are reacting to the changes introduced by the Government in the 1980s and 1990s. In the terms of this unit, severe constraints have been placed on their work, becoming operable through a 'managerialist discourse'. The authors claim that the teachers, in their response, are constructing their own discourse wherein they seek to preserve their own values.

Consider these questions as you read:

(a) What are the values underlying the government's planned reforms?

(b) What are the teachers' values, and how do they compare with those in (a)?

(c) What are the main features of the 'managerialist discourse'? How does it 'constrain' these teachers in their practice?

(d) What are the main features of the 'new professional discourse'? How successful do you consider these teachers to be in its construction, and how does it compare, in power terms, with the 'managerialist discourse'?

(e) How convincing do you find the arguments in the article? Attempt a brief critique.

Reading   (allow about 1 hour) ─────────────────────────────

Despite the problems noted in this unit, Alexander states that it 'ought to be possible to make questions about curriculum structure, classroom organization and teaching strategy much less ideologically fraught' (1992, p. 195), that is, less value-ridden. Please read Alexander 'In search of good primary practice' in Reader 2 (Woods), which is his attempt to devise such a model.

Consider the following questions as you read:

(a) What are some of the issues to be borne in mind when attempting to define 'good' teaching practice? Compare the points Alexander makes with those in this unit.

(b) How has 'good' primary practice, according to Alexander, been defined over the last twenty years, and with what consequences?

(c) How does Alexander define 'good practice'?

(d) How does the 'framework for conceptualizing practice' and the view of 'what is good practice' relate to the views of teaching advanced in Sections 2 and 3 of this unit?

(e) Attempt a critique of the article. How convincing do you find its arguments?

5   CONCLUSION

5.1   In this unit, two broad approaches to the issues of teachers' quality and teaching efficiency have been examined. Official reports do not question the social and political systems within which teaching takes place, nor the level of resource. They assume that the components of what constitutes good teaching are already known and see the main tasks as finding out how many measure up to it and devising policies about what to do with those they consider do not. The components of this ideal state of good teaching are never made explicit in the reports, but we looked at an attempt to draw out the major features. While some of these may be unremarkable and non-controversial, we saw that problems might arise in the connotations that might be put on some of them ('co-operative', for example, as contrasted with 'reformist'); on how they might be identified in practice; on their linkages with pupils' learning and, consequently, on their usefulness as an encouragement to good practice. Some might argue that they are more likely to induce stress among teachers, threatening to expose them to external forms of evaluation over which they have no control and through which they might experience what they see as unjustified sanctions. The DFEE might argue that they are mounting a responsible and determined drive to improve the quality of teaching in our schools. The analysis shows that this cannot be divorced from political considerations and the socio-economic context. That would help explain the emphasis on personal qualities and the demoting of other factors, such as headteachers' views and resource problems.

5.2   Teachers' values, interests and commitment were examined in Section 3. It was argued that in any consideration of teacher quality, a teacher's motivation and the factors influencing it have to be taken into consideration. It cannot be taken for granted. Similarly, the conditions (Section 4) within which teachers work might open up some lines of activity, but close down others. While there might be opportunities for teachers to exert some influences themselves on some of these factors (e.g. those connected with the institution), they have little control over some of the others, particularly those that arise from outside the school. In other respects, their values influence what they experience as constraint and what as opportunity. Teachers cope with what they experience as constraints typically through devising 'strategies'. Where the constraints are heavy, stress might be experienced. The greater incidence of stress among teachers since the 1988 Education Reform Act is indicated by the growing numbers of retirements through ill-health (5,549 under the age of 60 in 1993/4, 4,897 in 1992/3 compared to 2,551 in 1987/8 – the year before the Reform Act). Many of these teachers, arguably, have the highest 'personal qualities' (their strong ideals and total commitment not allowing them to compromise), and would be considered by many among the best teachers.

5.3   Where the constraints are few, teacher creativity is freer to flourish. On these occasions, teaching can seem like the expression of the true self.

> People who have not taught can have little idea what it is like to have *taught well* [author's italics], to be buoyed up and swept along by the response of students who are learning. One reaches for metaphors: chemical reactions, currents, setting alight, taking fire. But however difficult to describe … it is something that most teachers … have, at least some of the time.
>
> (Connell, 1985, p. 127.)

Now Connell's description is not unlike that of William James, in which he writes to his wife of the moments in which he feels 'most deeply and intensively active and alive [when] there is a voice inside which speaks and says, "This is the real me!"' … Perhaps it is in the precious moments when primary teachers become creative artists that they transcend the contradictions of the job and achieve the 'peak experience' … in which they, like James, become aware of their full identity.

(Nias, 1989, pp. 199–200.)

5.4   The two broad areas I have discussed, therefore, have had markedly different emphases, the first concentrating on teachers' personal qualities, the second on social factors. Yet a third, not discussed here, focuses on cognitive processes in teacher styles, and in matching tasks to pupils. While these at times are represented as competing explanations involving markedly different policy implications, I would argue that they do not have to be seen in that way and that all these elements are necessary for a comprehensive understanding of effective teaching, or indeed any sort of teaching. 'Opportunities to learn' are contingent upon 'opportunities to teach'. Cognitive matching needs to be seen within the context of social interaction and personal development. How teachers handle the complex issues raised within such a scenario very much depends on their personal knowledge, abilities, dispositions and skills. Better teaching would therefore involve both improved initial and in-service training of teachers and some other changes directed at constraints, especially the allocation of improved resources. This, arguably, would help promote a higher rate of matching within tasks on cognitive and on other dimensions.

5.5   There are at least two important factors that have been largely left out of account. One is, despite the references to teachers' subjectivities, the lack of involvement of teachers in the analysis. In the work considered in this unit, they are perceived as subjects of study, not as colleagues in the research. To see them as colleagues involves a policy change with regard to how these studies are tackled, if indeed the aim is the improvement of teaching (as opposed to a detached, academic analysis of it). Some people, therefore, are promoting 'action' research, whereby teachers examine their own practice, or 'collaborative' research, whereby teachers and researchers work together for mutual benefit (see, for example, Hustler *et al.*, 1986). Such an approach puts emphasis on improvement through heightened professionalism. This, again, could not take place in isolation from other policy aspects. Such activity, for example, would depend on teachers wishing to engage in it and having the time to do so.

5.6   The other factor largely omitted is the pupils. Like teachers, pupils' approaches to tasks, or school in general, are not only a matter of cognition, but are dependent upon motivation and aptitude, all of which are strongly influenced by a range of social factors. Furthermore, pupils do not just 'receive' teaching, but exert a considerable influence upon it themselves. This will be the subject of the next unit.

REFERENCES

ALEXANDER, R. J. (1992) *Policy and Practice in Primary Education*, London, Routledge.

ALEXANDER, R. J., ROSE, J. and WOODHEAD, C. (1992) *Curriculum Organisation and Classroom Practice in Primary Schools: a discussion paper*, London, Department of Education and Science, HMSO.

APPLE, M. W. (1986) *Teachers and Texts: a political economy of class and gender relations in education*, New York, Routledge and Kegan Paul.

APPLE, M. W. (1988) 'Work, class and teaching', in OZGA, J. (ed.) *Schoolwork: approaches to the labour process of teaching*, Milton Keynes, Open University Press.

APPLE, M. and JUNGCK, S. (1992) 'You don't have to be a teacher to teach this unit: teaching, technology and control in the curriculum', in HARGREAVES, A. and FULLAN, M. (eds.) *Understanding Teacher Development*, London, Cassell.

BALL, S. J. (1987) *The Micro-Politics of the School: towards a theory of school organizations*, London, Methuen.

BALL, S. J. and BOWE, R. (1992) 'Subject departments and the "implementation" of National Curriculum policy: an overview of the issues', *Journal of Curriculum Studies*, **24**(2), pp. 97–115.

BENNETT, N. (1976) *Teaching Styles and Pupil Progress*, London, Open Books.

BENNETT, N., DESFORGES, C., COCKBURN, A. and WILKINSON, B. (1984) *The Quality of Pupil Learning Experiences*, London, Lawrence Erlbaum.

BROADHEAD, P. (1987) 'A blueprint for the good teacher? The HMI/DES model of good primary practice', *British Journal of Educational Studies*, **35**(1), pp. 57–72.

CAMPBELL, R. J. (1993) 'The National Curriculum in primary schools: a dream at conception, a nightmare at delivery', in CHITTY, C. and SIMON, B. (eds) *Education Answers Back: critical responses to government policy*, London, Lawrence and Wishart.

CAMPBELL, R. J., EVANS, L., NEILL, S. R. ST. J. and PACKWOOD, A. (1991) *Workloads, Achievements and Stress: two follow-up studies of teacher time in Key Stage 1*, Warwick, Policy Analysis Unit, Department of Education, University of Warwick.

CAMPBELL, R. J., EVANS, L., NEILL, S. R. ST. J. and PACKWOOD, A. (1991a) 'The use and management of infant teachers' time – some policy issues', paper presented at Policy Analysis Unit Seminar, Department of Education, University of Warwick, November.

CENTRAL ADVISORY COUNCIL FOR EDUCATION (ENGLAND) (CACE) (1967) *Children and Their Primary Schools*, London, HMSO (The Plowden Report).

CONNELL, R. W. (1985) *Teachers' Work*, London, Allen and Unwin.

DENSCOMBE, M. (1980) 'Keeping 'em quiet: the significance of noise for the practical activity of teaching', in WOODS, P. (ed.) *Teacher Strategies*, London, Croom Helm.

DENSCOMBE, M. (1985) *Classroom Control: a sociological perspective*, London, Allen and Unwin.

DENSMORE, K. (1987) 'Professionalism, proletarianisation and teachers' work', in POPKEWITZ, T. (ed.) *Critical Studies in Teacher Education*, Lewes, Falmer Press.

DEPARTMENT OF EDUCATION AND SCIENCE (DES) (1982) *The New Teacher in School*, London, HMSO.

DEPARTMENT OF EDUCATION AND SCIENCE (DES) (1983) *Teaching Quality*, London, HMSO.

DEPARTMENT OF EDUCATION AND SCIENCE (DES) (1985) *Better Schools*, London, HMSO.

DEPARTMENT OF EDUCATION AND SCIENCE (DES) (1985a) *Education Observed 3 – Good Teachers*, London, HMSO.

DEPARTMENT OF EDUCATION AND SCIENCE (DES) (1986) *Report by Her Majesty's Inspectors on the Effects of Local Authority Expenditure Policies on Education Provision in England – 1985*, London, HMSO.

DRUMMOND, M. J. (1991) 'The child and the primary curriculum – from policy to practice', *The Curriculum Journal*, **2**(2), pp. 115–24.

ELBAZ, F. (1992) 'Hope, attentiveness, and caring for difference: the moral voice in teaching', *Teaching and Teacher Education*, **8**(5/6), pp. 411–32.

GALTON, M., SIMON, B., and CROLL, P. (1980) *Inside the Primary Classroom*, London, Routledge and Kegan Paul.

HARGREAVES, A. (1994) *Changing Teachers, Changing Times*, London, Cassell.

HARTLEY, D. (1985) *Understanding the Primary School: a sociological analysis*, London, Croom Helm.

HUSTLER, D. *et al.* (1986) *Action Research in Classrooms and Schools*, London, Allen and Unwin.

LACEY, C. (1977) *The Socialization of Teachers*, London, Methuen.

LAWTON, D. (1987) 'Teaching quality, quality teaching and the culture of the school: the 1986 SERA lecture', *Scottish Educational Review*, **19**(1), pp. 3–12.

MAC AN GHAILL, M. (1992) 'Teachers' work: curriculum restructuring, culture, power and comprehensive schooling', *British Journal of Sociology of Education*, **13**(2), pp. 177–99.

MAC AN GHAILL, M. (1992a) 'Student perspectives on curriculum innovation and change in an English secondary school: an empirical study', *British Educational Research Journal*, **18**(3), pp. 221–34.

MCNAMARA, D. (1986) 'The personal qualities of the teacher and educational policy: a critique', *British Educational Research Journal*, **12**(1), pp. 29–36.

NIAS, J. (1981) 'Commitment and motivation in primary school teachers', *Educational Review*, **33**(3), pp. 181–90.

NIAS, J. (1989) *Primary Teachers Talking: a study of teaching as work*, London, Routledge.

NIAS, J. (1991) 'Changing times, changing identities: grieving for a lost self', in BURGESS, R. G. (ed.) *Educational Research and Evaluation*, London, Falmer Press.

NIAS, J., SOUTHWORTH, G. and CAMPBELL, P. (1992) *Whole School Curriculum Development in the Primary School*, London, Falmer Press.

OFSTED (1992) *The Handbook for the Inspection of Schools*, London, Office for Standards in Education.

OFSTED (1994) *Primary Matters*, London, Office for Standards in Education.

OSBORN, M., BROADFOOT, P., POLLARD, A., CROLL, P. and ABBOTT, D. (1994) 'Teachers' professional perspectives: continuity and change', Paper presented as part of Symposium, *Managing Change in the Primary School*, CEDAR International Conference, University of Warwick, April 1994.

POLLARD, A. (1992) 'Teachers' responses to the reshaping of primary education', in ARNOT, M. and BARTON, L. (eds) *Voicing Concerns*, London, Triangle Books.

POLLARD, A., BROADFOOT, P., CROLL, P., OSBORN, M. and ABBOTT, D. (1994) *Changing English Primary Schools? The impact of the Education Reform Act at key stage one*, London, Cassell.

RISEBOROUGH, G. F. (1981) 'Teacher careers and comprehensive school: an empirical study', *Sociology*, **15**(3), pp. 352–81.

ROEHLER, L. R. and DUFFY, G. G. (1986) 'What makes one teacher a better explainer than another', *Journal of Education for Teaching*, **12**(3), pp. 273–84.

RUTTER, M., MAUGHAM, B., MORTIMORE, P. and OUSTON, J. (1979) *Fifteen Thousand Hours*, London, Open Books.

SHARP, R. and GREEN, A. (1975) *Education and Social Control*, London, Routledge and Kegan Paul.

SIKES, P., MEASOR, L. and WOODS, P. (1985) *Teacher Careers: crises and continuities*, Lewes, Falmer Press.

TOM, A. (1988) 'Teaching as a moral craft', in DALE, R., FERGUSSON, R. and ROBINSON, A. (eds.) *Frameworks for Teaching*, London, Hodder and Stoughton.

VERNON, M. (1986) 'A burnt out case', *The Times Educational Supplement*, 31 January 1986, p. 21.

WOODS, P. (1979) *The Divided School*, London, Routledge and Kegan Paul.

WRAGG, E. (1991) *Mad Curriculum Disease*, Stoke-on-Trent, Trentham Books.

EU208 Exploring Educational Issues

BLOCK 1   INTRODUCTION
BLOCK 2   FAMILY AND SCHOOL
BLOCK 3   TEACHING AND LEARNING
BLOCK 4   ORGANIZATION AND CONTROL OF SCHOOLING
BLOCK 5   EQUALITY AND EDUCATION
BLOCK 6   EDUCATION, WORK AND SOCIAL CHANGE
BLOCK 7   EDUCATION IN EUROPE